Original title:
Winter's Promise

Copyright © 2024 Swan Charm
All rights reserved.

Author: Liisi Lendorav
ISBN HARDBACK: 978-9916-79-618-4
ISBN PAPERBACK: 978-9916-79-619-1
ISBN EBOOK: 978-9916-79-620-7

Hidden Warmth in the White Out

In the blanket of snow, stillness reigns,
Beneath, the earth whispers, softly retains.
Echoes of life in the cold, dark night,
Hidden warmth glimmers, just out of sight.

Branches heavy, dressed in icy lace,
Yet beneath the surface, memories trace.
The heartbeat of seasons, a secret to keep,
Where dreams find shelter, and silence sleeps.

Shadows dance lightly, in twilight's embrace,
In the hush of the winter, a magical space.
Around every corner, a promise of light,
Life stirs in the shadows, ready for flight.

Though the world seems barren, the spirit endures,
Whispers of green through the cold, it assures.
Nature's soft hand, a caress from above,
Hiding the warmth, wrapped in pure love.

The Unseen Spring Beneath the Snow

Under layers of frost, the earth holds its breath,
Life waits in silence, beyond the cold death.
Buds cling to branches, patient and still,
Ready to burst forth, with the sun's gentle thrill.

Hidden are colors in the monochrome white,
A symphony brewing, out of our sight.
Whispers of warmth in the chill of the air,
Nature's soft magic, it's everywhere.

Drifted upon snow, seeds dream of the day,
When the sun's golden rays chase the winter away.
A tapestry woven in quietude deep,
The unseen spring stirs, in a dreamful sleep.

With each passing moment, the ice starts to break,
Life's gentle promise, not far from awake.
Pushing through layers, with fervor and grace,
The unseen spring smiles, ready to embrace.

Nature's Quiet Rebirth

In the hush of the dawn, a slow awakening,
Nature reflects on what life is bringing.
Gentle buds stretching, reaching for light,
Painting the world in colors so bright.

The whispering winds carry tales from the past,
Of seasons gone by, yet their shadows last.
With each drop of dew, a promise is made,
Of vibrant blooms born from the cool, soft shade.

A chorus of creatures begins to emerge,
From depths of the earth, they slowly converge.
With birds softly singing, and leaves in a dance,
Nature's rebirth gives us all a chance.

Each blade of grass, each petal and bud,
Reflects the rhythm of life in the mud.
In every corner, fresh stories are spun,
Two worlds intertwine, as they greet the sun.

Echoing Laughter in the Cold

In the crisp air, laughter rolls,
Children's voices, joyous, whole.
Snowflakes dance from the dark sky,
Echoes linger, as time slips by.

Footprints mark the white expanse,
As winter's chill invites a chance.
To share warmth beneath the stars,
Where dreams are whispered, near and far.

Sleds race down the gleaming hill,
Hearts are light, the world stands still.
In every giggle, memories wait,
Bound by laughter, we celebrate.

Lanterns in the Snow

Flickering lights on a winter's night,
Lanterns gleam, a soft delight.
Guiding paths through the snowy lanes,
Whispers of hope, love remains.

Each glow tells stories of old,
Of warmth and joy, brave and bold.
Against the frost and darkened sky,
They bloom like dreams that dare to fly.

Beneath their shine, we gather near,
Sharing laughter, shedding fear.
A tapestry of warmth implores,
As night unfolds, our spirit soars.

The Hearth's Silent Call

In the quiet, embers glow,
The hearth's warmth, a gentle flow.
Timeless tales in curling smoke,
The silence speaks, the heart awoke.

Cloaked in shadows, friends unite,
Beneath the mantle's soft, sweet light.
Crackling sounds, like whispered sighs,
The hearth's call draws us, never dies.

A gathering place, where hearts reside,
In every flicker, love won't hide.
We weave our stories, tales we hold,
In the warmth of the fire, our truths unfold.

Frostbitten but Not Broken

Beneath the weight of winter's grasp,
The chill bites deep, a frigid clasp.
Yet within the heart, a fire stays,
Frostbitten dreams continue to blaze.

Resilient souls, we rise and fight,
With every step, we find the light.
Through icy paths and bitter nights,
Our spirits soar, reclaiming heights.

Icicles hang like frozen tears,
Yet laughter cuts through all our fears.
We walk on, brave, never alone,
In unity, our strength has grown.

Whispers Beneath the Ice

In silent depths, the secrets lie,
Beneath the frost, where shadows sigh.
Frozen tales, in cold embrace,
Whispers of time, they leave no trace.

Echoes dance in chilly air,
Memories trapped, held with care.
Crystals gleam with stories old,
Quiet truths, in silence told.

Beneath the surface, life awaits,
Nature's pulse, it thrums and vibrates.
Patience waits for spring's sweet call,
To awaken all, in warmth they'll sprawl.

Whispers merge with thawing tide,
In the sun's glow, secrets bide.
As layers peel, the past unfolds,
In every crack, a story holds.

Beneath the ice, all is still,
Yet life persists, an unseen will.
In frozen depths, we find our grace,
Embracing time, a soft embrace.

Stars Beneath the Snow

Under the hush of winter's glow,
The heavens arch where cold winds blow.
Stars twinkle bright, like jewels rare,
In a blanket of white, beyond compare.

Each flake falls, a whispered dream,
Glimmers caught in a silver beam.
Night unfolds its velvet cloak,
As distant worlds in silence spoke.

In moonlit realms, the shadows play,
Guiding lost souls on their way.
Radiant wishes, a soft delight,
Stars illuminate the frosty night.

Beneath the snow, great stories sleep,
In frozen sighs, their secrets keep.
Awakening soon, when spring arrives,
To dance once more, where each heart thrives.

Whispers of stardust softly sway,
In winter's hold, they softly lay.
Beneath the snow, life still breathes,
Creating magic in gentle wreaths.

The Promise of Returning Light

In the depths of winter's night,
Hope flickers dim, yet holds its light.
Days grow short, shadows expand,
Yet whispers promise, so gently planned.

Every dawn brings warmth anew,
Painting skies in brightening hue.
A journey forged through frost and chill,
With every step, we bend our will.

The sun will rise, the darkness yield,
Nature's canvas, a vibrant field.
With every ray, the heart rejoices,
In stillness, we find hopeful voices.

Buds will bloom from icy ground,
Life awakens, beauty found.
What once lay still now starts to stir,
In the promise of light, we confer.

Chains of cold begin to break,
As warmth returns, the earth will wake.
In the glow of day, shadows flee,
The promise of light sets our souls free.

Sledding Through Secrets

Down the hill, with laughter's sound,
Sleds rush forth, on snow they bound.
Secrets whispered through the breeze,
Each glide a thrill, life's perfect tease.

Winter's chill wraps the landscape tight,
Creating joy in pure delight.
With every turn, stories unfold,
Adventure waits, both brave and bold.

We chase the thrill of icy runs,
Beneath the gaze of fading suns.
In sparkling snow, a world so wide,
With friends beside, we all abide.

Each bump and dip, a heart's quick race,
Through frosty air, we find our place.
Sledding down, we leave our cares,
In winter's arms, freedom flares.

Nature's canvas, white and bright,
Hopes and dreams in each sledding flight.
Through laughter shared, the secrets blend,
Moments we cherish, that never end.

Cradled in the Chill

Beneath a sky of whispers,
The frost begins to creep.
A world wrapped in a silence,
Where shadows gently sleep.

The breath of winter's magic,
Invites the stars to twinkle.
Each flake a silver secret,
In glistening dreams that sprinkle.

The night air holds a moment,
Where time seems to stand still.
Cradled in the chill of night,
A heart learns how to feel.

Soft echoes of the evening,
Dance lightly on the breeze.
While the moon collects the dreams,
That flutter 'mongst the trees.

As dawn begins to whisper,
The hues of gold arise.
Cradled in the chill we found,
The beauty of the skies.

Silence of the Snowflakes

In the hush of falling flakes,
A world begins to fade.
Each flake a tiny whisper,
A promise softly made.

They blanket all in softness,
A gentle, quiet grace.
Silent moments linger,
In this frosty, timeless place.

The laughter of the children,
Breaks through the icy air.
While snowflakes spin like dancers,
Their joy beyond compare.

A tapestry of silence,
Weaves dreams upon the ground.
In the peace of winter's heart,
Love's quiet voice is found.

Through the white-blanketed woods,
Nature hums a tune.
The silence of the snowflakes,
A soothing winter's croon.

Dreams Adrift on a Frozen Lake

Beneath the frosted surface,
A stillness echoes deep.
Dreams adrift on frozen waves,
In slumber, softly sleep.

The stars reflect like lanterns,
In the night's calm embrace.
While winter's breath feels gentle,
Time gathers at this place.

Cold winds brush through the branches,
A lullaby so sweet.
A moment shared in silence,
As hearts and dreams compete.

Each ripple holds a story,
Of laughter, love, and light.
Dreams adrift on frozen lakes,
Dance softly in the night.

In the crystal-coated world,
Hope glimmers like the dawn.
Our dreams, adrift and floating,
In endless winter's song.

Tired Trees Resting

Beneath the weight of snowflakes,
The tired trees stand tall.
In quiet contemplation,
They hear the winter's call.

Branches arch like weary arms,
Seeking a gentle sigh.
Wrapped in cool and silver light,
Underneath the cobalt sky.

Each tree tells a story,
Of seasons passed and gone.
Their roots hold whispered secrets,
As they greet each dusky dawn.

In the stillness of the forest,
They sway with winter's tune.
Tired trees, they find their solace,
In the embrace of the moon.

So let the snowflakes cover them,
In a blanket soft and white.
Tired trees, forever cradled,
Awaiting spring's warm light.

The Heartbeat of Midwinter

In the chill where silence breathes,
Snowflakes dance on the winter's eaves.
Whispers carry through the night,
Stars glimmer with a distant light.

Branches drape in white attire,
Hidden dreams in cold aspire.
A distant echo, warmth confined,
Heartbeat knows what love can find.

Footsteps crunch on virgin ground,
In the stillness, peace is found.
Midwinter's grasp, so tight, so bright,
Bears the hope of spring's first light.

Embers glow in shadows play,
Fireside tales of yesterday.
Heartfelt laughter fills the air,
In every glance, a venture rare.

When the sun returns once more,
Midwinter's gifts we will adore.
For in this frozen, radiant sea,
Lies the pulse of memory.

Secrets of the Frostbound Heart

Beneath layers of icy skin,
Quiet yearnings stir within.
Every flake a tale untold,
Hidden warmth keeps secrets bold.

In the freeze, where dreams take flight,
Hope lingers in the longest night.
Breeze carries whispers of the past,
Through glistening branches, shadows cast.

Frostbound heart, a timeless dance,
Awaiting spring, it dares to chance.
With every dawn, a fragile sigh,
Promises woven in the sky.

In the silence, echoes bloom,
From the darkness, life finds room.
Secret gardens waiting, still,
Underneath the winter's chill.

Hear the pulse beneath the freeze,
Nature murmurs through the trees.
The frostbound heart knows its way,
Guided by the light of day.

Frosted Whispers

In the stillness, secrets lie,
Snowflakes fall as time drifts by.
Frosted whispers in the air,
Gentle moments, love laid bare.

Under blankets, soft and warm,
Gentle hearts begin to charm.
Every breath, a silent song,
In winter's hold, where dreams belong.

Trees wear coats of icy lace,
Twinkling lights, a gleaming grace.
Moonlit paths where shadows play,
Frosted whispers guide the way.

Through the night, where peace descends,
Nature rests, and time transcends.
With the dawn, new stories weave,
Frosted whispers we believe.

In this world of silver sheen,
Every heartbeat feels serene.
In winter's soft embrace we find,
Frosted whispers, intertwined.

Beneath the Snow's Embrace

In the depth of winter's hold,
Stories of the heart unfold.
Snowflakes weave a quiet tale,
Underneath, the spirits sail.

Every branch bears weight of white,
Crafting dreams in the moonlight.
Beneath the snow, life sleeps and waits,
For spring's kiss to reveal fates.

Underneath the icy seam,
Every pulse holds a secret dream.
Nature whispers soft and low,
In the calm, the feelings flow.

Crisp and clear, the morning breaks,
Awakening the scene that shakes.
Beneath the snow, a heart beats strong,
A symphony, where we belong.

When thaw returns with gentle grace,
Life will rise from winter's embrace.
Every heartbeat, brave and true,
Blooms anew in morning's hue.

Embracing the Cold

The winter wind whispers low,
Embracing the chill, we go.
Frosted breaths dance in the air,
Nature's beauty, stark and rare.

Snowflakes waltz through silent nights,
Blanketing earth in soft white lights.
Timeless peace in frozen tones,
Hearts find warmth in winter's homes.

Sipping cocoa by the fire,
Memories stoked, dreams inspire.
Woolen blankets snugly wrapped,
In this stillness, joy is tapped.

The world slows down under stars,
Each twinkle reminds us who we are.
Seasons change, yet here we stay,
Embracing warmth in cold's embrace.

In the quiet, we find our soul,
Winter's touch makes us feel whole.
With each breath, hope takes its hold,
Together we brave the bitter cold.

Shadows of Shorter Days

As daylight fades, shadows creep,
Lengthening nights that pull us deep.
Golden hues retreat in haste,
Fragrant air of harvest's taste.

Crisp leaves rustle underfoot,
Time to gather, time to root.
Silent whispers of the trees,
Echo softly in the breeze.

Fires crackle, stories share,
Gathered close, love's warmth laid bare.
Laughter lingers in the air,
In these moments, life feels fair.

The clock ticks slow, the world holds still,
Wrapped in twilight, hearts can fill.
Finding solace in the night,
Holding close the fading light.

Seasons shift, but we remain,
Through the shadows, love's refrain.
Embracing what the dusk bestows,
Together facing winter's snows.

Wistful Icicles

Icicles hang from rooftops tall,
Glistening jewels in the chill's thrall.
Lazy drips form puddles below,
In their beauty, time moves slow.

Each shard a memory encased,
Whispers of winter's icy grace.
Fragile, delicate, they shine bright,
Reflecting dreams in soft twilight.

Nature's art, so breathtaking fine,
A fleeting moment, a fragile line.
As sunlight warms the frozen ground,
Wistful thoughts dance all around.

With every thaw, a change will come,
Life awakens, winter's hum.
Yet in the heart, they softly cling,
Reminders of what cold can bring.

In the melting, beauty lies,
Lessons learned under winter skies.
The promise kept, as seasons sway,
Wistful icicles fade away.

The Promise of Thaw

Beneath the snow, the earth sleeps tight,
Dreaming of spring and morning light.
Whispers of warmth begin to play,
The promise of thaw, a brand new day.

Tulips peek through drifts of white,
As sunbeams break the quiet night.
Birds return with songs anew,
Nature awakens, fresh and true.

Streams trickle, laughter in the air,
Life returns with vibrant flair.
Colors burst, a canvas bright,
Every shade, pure delight.

Hope unfurls in gentle sun,
Life renews, we've just begun.
In the thaw, we shed our fears,
Welcome change with open cheers.

The cycle turns, a dance we know,
In every ending, beginnings grow.
With every bloom, our hearts will sigh,
For in the thaw, we learn to fly.

Hibernation's Lull

In the stillness of the night,
Creatures nestle in their plight.
Wrapped in dreams, they softly sigh,
Nature's breath, a whispered lullaby.

Snowflakes dance upon the ground,
A tranquil peace, so profound.
Silent woods in slumber deep,
Guard the secrets that they keep.

Winter's coat, a heavy veil,
Cradles life, with tender tale.
Hearts beat slow in this embrace,
Time itself finds quieter pace.

Beneath the stars, the world is calm,
In the chaos, there's a balm.
Hibernation's gentle sway,
Guides us through the coldest day.

Embers Beneath the Ice

Beneath the frost, the warmth still glows,
A quiet fire that gently flows.
Hidden sparks in frozen ground,
Life persists, though silence found.

Icicles hang like moments frail,
Time suspended, wind's frail wail.
Yet under layers, hearts conspire,
To awaken from the coldest fire.

The breath of spring begins to tease,
A promise whispered in the breeze.
As shadows play on gleaming white,
Embers wait for dawn's first light.

In crystalline realms, dreams entwine,
Where warmth is tracked through pure design.
Though winter's grip is cold and tight,
Hope flickers softly, burning bright.

Lanterns in the Frost

In the dark, the lanterns gleam,
Guiding lost souls through the dream.
Frosted paths that spark and glow,
A magical world covered in snow.

Each flicker tells a tale unknown,
Of whispered wishes and seeds sown.
Under stars, the journey unfolds,
With every light, a story told.

Glimmers pierce the chilly night,
Casting shadows, chasing fright.
Beneath the chill, the spirits rise,
Lanterns wink with knowing eyes.

As dawn approaches, hues of gold,
Replace the silver, crisp and bold.
In every frost, a promise made,
That warmth returns, the night's charade.

A Pact with the Chill

In the heart of winter's grasp,
We make a deal, a careful clasp.
To dance with frost, to laugh with snow,
For in the chill, we learn to grow.

The air bites sharp, but we endure,
Find solace in the cold, the pure.
With every breath, a vow we take,
To embrace the stillness, for beauty's sake.

The world transformed in icy lace,
Nature dons a crystal face.
Together we wander, hand in hand,
Through frozen fields, a land so grand.

Whispers of wind, a solemn pact,
In winter's heart, we find our act.
For every frost that may fall,
There's warmth within, a welcoming call.

Beneath the Jacket of Ice

Beneath the jacket of ice, cold and white,
Whispers of warmth dance through the night.
Silent the world, but hearts still beat,
Dreams wrapped in frost, yet never complete.

Shadows of winter cast long and wide,
Hidden from light, where secrets reside.
Beneath the surface, life still flows,
Gathering strength where no one knows.

Time ticks slowly, in layers of chill,
Mirrored reflections on windows, still.
Frozen pathways lead to the dark,
Hope lingers gently, igniting a spark.

Under the moon's soft, silvery glow,
Nature breathes deep, where no winds blow.
Amidst the freeze, resilience shines bright,
A tapestry woven of purest light.

So under the frost, dreams gently lie,
Waiting for warmth as the seasons sigh.
Beneath the jacket of ice, hidden grace,
Nature holds secrets in her embrace.

The Lullaby of Long Nights

The lullaby of long nights softly sings,
Stars twinkle gently, on crystal wings.
In the stillness, shadows blend and play,
Whispers of peace at the end of the day.

Moonlight pours like silver upon the ground,
Enveloping silence, a soothing sound.
Wrapped in the depths of a starry quilt,
Hearts find tranquility, where hope is built.

Every heartbeat echoes, a rhythmic tune,
Under the watchful eye of the moon.
Dreams wander freely, like leaves in the breeze,
Carried away to the land of ease.

Crisp air fills the lungs, a refreshing sigh,
While the world pauses, as night draws nigh.
In the embrace of the endless dark sky,
Every moment whispers a gentle goodbye.

As night grows older, and dreams take flight,
The lullaby fades, welcoming bright light.
For in every ending, a new day will start,
Bringing forth warmth, and a hopeful heart.

Glimmers of Hope in the Frost

Glimmers of hope in the frost appear,
A dance of light, brightening the drear.
Among the crystals, dreams spark and gleam,
A canvas of ice, where wishes redeem.

The chill wraps around like a subtle embrace,
While warmth fights back, claiming its space.
Beneath the frost, life finds a way,
In shadows of winter, hope dances and sways.

Every flake tells a story, unique and bright,
In the depths of the freeze, flickers of light.
Nature's resilience in silence reveals,
The glimmers of hope, which winter conceals.

So let the cold wind howl and take flight,
Even in darkness, the spirit ignites.
For those little glimmers, so bold and so sweet,
Show that in struggle, life can't be beat.

With every dawn, the frost starts to melt,
The warmth of the sun is eagerly felt.
Glimmers of hope, in the frost, shall don,
A promise of spring, in the light of the dawn.

Blooming in the Deep Freeze

Blooming in the deep freeze, life holds tight,
Against the odds, it seeks the light.
Petals unfurl with a delicate grace,
In the stillness of winter, they find their place.

Icicles glisten like jewels on a vine,
Bravely defying, with a rhythm divine.
Each bud a testament to nature's art,
Resilience woven in every heart.

Beneath the snow, the seeds gently sleep,
Waiting for warmth, their dreams to keep.
Through whispers of cold, they silently yearn,
For the sun's warm embrace, for the spring tide's return.

Even in frost, beauty emerges,
In the harshest of trials, hope surges.
Blooming in places where few dare to go,
Color bursts forth, like a vibrant glow.

With patience as armor, they push through the freeze,
Nature's bold promise, instilling unease.
For in every winter, life's lessons reprise,
A bloom in the frost, a wonder that flies.

A Nurtured Slumber

In quiet night, the world does breathe,
A gentle hush falls upon the leaves.
Stars above with twinkling light,
Whispers dreams through velvet night.

Cradled soft in nature's fold,
Hope awaits in silken gold.
Time drifts by without a care,
While moonlight casts a tranquil glare.

Each creature finds a place to rest,
Wrapped in warmth, their hearts are blessed.
The earth prepares for days anew,
As morning sun brings life in view.

A slumber deep, a cycle grand,
When nature sleeps, it makes its stand.
In dreams of green and vibrant hue,
Life awakens, fresh and true.

The Frozen Breath of Nature

A silver mist upon the ground,
Each breath of frost, a quiet sound.
Trees wear coats of crystal white,
Nature rests in purest light.

Rivers pause in sparkling sleep,
Wrapped in blankets cold and deep.
Birds take hush in silent flight,
The world transformed, so pure, so bright.

Mountains echo with a sigh,
Underneath the frozen sky.
Blades of grass, a glittering sheet,
Nature's art, both cold and sweet.

Days grow short, but hearts expand,
In this peace, we understand.
Winter's breath a promise made,
Of spring's return, in sun and shade.

Beneath the Blanket of Ice

Beneath the ice, life stirs and dreams,
Hidden realms, where silence screams.
Roots entwined in slumber deep,
Awaits the time for life to leap.

Nature's quilt, so cold yet bright,
Woven with the stars at night.
Frozen lakes, a mirror still,
Reflecting all of winter's chill.

Within the frost, the seeds remain,
Caught in a delicate chain.
The world outside, a crystal play,
While life prepares for brighter day.

In shadows cast by silver moon,
Dreams of spring will blossom soon.
A heartbeat hidden, deep within,
Awaiting warmth to spark again.

The Resilience of Dormant Seeds

Within the earth, the seeds reside,
Dormant dreams in soil abide.
Wrapped in whispers, soft and low,
Awaiting sun and gentle snow.

Prophecies in shells of brown,
The strength of life will wear the crown.
Through darkest nights and harshest storms,
The heart of life forever warms.

In time, a crack, a hint of green,
Emerging from the cool and serene.
With tender roots that reach and crave,
Seeds rise up from their silent grave.

Resilient hearts will find their way,
Each blossom tells of yesterday.
Through seasons' change, they'll stand and sing,
Of all the hope that spring can bring.

Breathing in the Stillness

In the quiet, whispers bloom,
Softly lingers, a gentle gloom.
Time suspended, moments freeze,
Nature sighs with tender ease.

Stars awaken, shadows grow,
Moonlight dances, soft and slow.
In this pause, the heart can hear,
Tranquil thoughts, crystal clear.

Branches sway with whispered song,
In the silence, we belong.
Presence felt in every breath,
Life unfolds, untouched by death.

Breathe in deep the stillness near,
Nurtured by each calming sphere.
In this space where time will bend,
Find the peace that knows no end.

Chasing Snowflakes

Falling softly from the sky,
Dancing gently, drifting by.
Laughter echoes in the chill,
Resting softly on the hill.

Each a gem, a fleeting grace,
Whirling down in wild embrace.
Children rush with open arms,
Capturing their fleeting charms.

In the air, a frosty breath,
Whispers tales of winter's breadth.
Joyful moments, lost in flight,
Chasing dreams of purest white.

The world transformed, a wonderland,
Where imagination takes a stand.
We catch these flakes, then let go,
In the magic of the snow.

Beneath the Crystal Canopy

Trees adorned in glistening white,
Underneath, a world of light.
Branches bow with weight so grand,
Nature's beauty, softly planned.

Whispers echo in the air,
Creating moments, pure and rare.
Footsteps crunch on frosty ground,
In this stillness, love is found.

Crystal drops like hidden gems,
Lighting up the forest hems.
In this refuge, hearts align,
Time slows down, the stars all shine.

Above us, dreams like snowflakes fall,
Wrapping nature in a shawl.
Beneath this canopy so fair,
Feel the magic everywhere.

In silence, wonders intertwine,
Writing stories, yours and mine.
Underneath this crystal dome,
In nature, we feel at home.

Solstice Reflections

Shadows lengthen, daylight fades,
In this stillness, time cascades.
Winter whispers, secrets shared,
In the heart, we feel prepared.

Moments pause, the world holds breath,
Beauty found in whispered depth.
Firelight flickers, warmth displayed,
Memories dance in light and shade.

With each sunset, we reflect,
On the dreams that we collect.
Holding close what brings us peace,
In these moments, we find release.

Solstice magic in the air,
Caught between despair and care.
In this twilight, let us speak,
Gather strength, we find the peak.

Through the dark, the world will turn,
In our hearts, the embers burn.
Hope ignites; we'll rise again,
In the cycle, love remains.

Slumbering Lands

In fields of green, the shadows lie,
Where whispers drift and softly sigh.
Beneath the trees, the memories fade,
In dreams of night, the light cascades.

Mountains steep, they stand so grand,
Guardians of this ancient land.
With every breeze, the secrets flow,
Where rivers gleam, and wildflowers grow.

Underneath the pale moon's glow,
Awakening hearts begin to know.
The starry sky, a vast embrace,
In slumbering lands, we find our place.

The tales of old in silence sing,
In gentle hum of early spring.
Each pause of life, a sacred thread,
In every dream, where hope is fed.

So let us wander, hand in hand,
Through midnight realms of this soft land.
In slumbering lands, we'll remain still,
With promises, our hearts will fill.

The Frost's Embrace

In winter's grasp, the world is still,
A quiet peace on every hill.
The icy breath that coats the night,
As stars above burn pure and bright.

Frozen lakes like mirrors lay,
Reflecting dreams that drift away.
A blanket white, the trees adorn,
In beauty's chill, the earth reborn.

The laughter of the wind is clear,
In every flake, it draws us near.
With every step on crunching snow,
The world of ice begins to glow.

Beneath the frost, life holds its breath,
As nature sings of hidden depths.
In chilly nights, we find our grace,
Warm in the frost's enchanting embrace.

So let us walk through winter's spell,
In the embrace where silence dwells.
With hearts aglow, we brave the cold,
In tales of frost, our journey unfolds.

Hushed Twilight

As day gives way to evening's hue,
The sky transforms to deepest blue.
In softest whisper, stars appear,
Each twinkle drawing dreams so near.

The trees stand tall, a silent choir,
Their branches dance with soft desire.
In twilight's glow, the shadows creep,
A moment's pause before night's deep.

The air is filled with scents of fall,
As daylight starts its final call.
With each heartbeat, the world awakes,
To secrets that the twilight makes.

In the stillness, time seems to bend,
As day and night become close friends.
A tranquil space, where spirits fly,
In hushed twilight, the dreams comply.

So let us bask in fading light,
Where moments linger, calm and bright.
In this embrace, we find our way,
Through hushed twilight, to the end of day.

Icy Anthems

In winter's grip, a silence reigns,
The world adorned in crystal chains.
Each flake a note, a song divine,
Composed in whispers, every line.

The breath of cold commands the air,
A symphony beyond compare.
In icy realms, the echoes rise,
As magic twinkles in the skies.

With every gust, the anthems play,
And dancers twirl as shadows sway.
The moonlit path, a melody,
In frozen dreams, we wander free.

The branches sway, they hum in tune,
Beneath the watchful, glowing moon.
A world united, hearts ablaze,
In icy anthems, we find our ways.

So let us celebrate the night,
With sparkling stars, our guiding light.
Through winter's song, we'll boldly press,
In icy anthems, we find our rest.

Glimmers in the Gloom

In shadows deep, the light does creep,
Flickers faint, yet secrets keep.
Silver beams on silent ground,
Hope's reflection can be found.

Amidst the dark, a spark does shine,
Whispers of days when all was fine.
Each moment counts, each breath a gift,
In twilight's grasp, our spirits lift.

The night may cloak, but hearts still burn,
Lessons learned, and tides that turn.
Bright constellations guide our way,
Through the dusk, into the day.

A gentle touch of evening's grace,
Kindred souls in quiet space.
Together we face the lurking dread,
Seeking light that gently spread.

Whispers of Renewal

Beneath the frost, the earth does yearn,
To feel the warmth, for life to turn.
Softest breezes carry dreams,
Awakening the ancient streams.

The buds unfold with colors bright,
As nature sings of pure delight.
Every leaf, a tale untold,
In whispers soft, a journey bold.

Through winter's grasp, we find our way,
Seeds of hope in soil lay.
Beneath the stars, new paths arise,
In every heart, the sun will rise.

Eager hands plant visions clear,
Tending to all we hold dear.
With every dawn, a chance to grow,
In whispers, life begins to flow.

The Art of Stillness

In quiet hours, the mind takes flight,
Finding peace in serene night.
With gentle breaths, the chaos fades,
In stillness, clarity invades.

Moments stretch like endless seas,
Softly caught in whispering breeze.
Time pauses, dreams intertwine,
In silence, our souls align.

Thoughts like clouds drift softly by,
Underneath the vast, blue sky.
A meditative dance we weave,
In every pause, we learn to breathe.

Embrace the calm, let worries cease,
In stillness, we unearth our peace.
In quiet spaces, spirits mend,
Finding solace, without end.

Threads of Ice

Crystalline whispers on winter's breath,
Fragile beauty, skirting death.
Treading lightly on glistening fields,
Nature's art, her grace reveals.

Frosted branches, delicate lace,
In shimmering stillness, we find our place.
Each flake a story, unique and rare,
Frozen whispers dance in the air.

Time seems to pause in the chilling air,
Thoughts like snowflakes, floating with care.
Through icy realms, we wander wide,
Finding warmth where hearts abide.

Beneath the chill, a spark ignites,
In winter's hold, we share our lights.
Threads of ice, a fragile thread,
Binding us close in the silence ahead.

The Hidden Life Below

In the quiet earth below,
Whispers stir in roots that grow.
Mice and beetles hide from light,
Life abounds, a secret sight.

Underneath the surface deep,
Ancient tales in silence sleep.
Tiny worlds in shadows creep,
Nature's pulse, a rhythm to keep.

Through the soil, life finds its way,
Dancing in the dark of day.
Fungi weave a soft embrace,
Nurturing the hidden space.

Streams of moisture gently flow,
Where the hidden creatures sow.
Life beneath the heavy ground,
In the stillness, peace is found.

Seasons change, as roots entwine,
In the dark, the sun does shine.
All around, the cycle spins,
In the depths, the hidden wins.

Glacial Enchantment

A world of ice, so pure, so grand,
Frozen dreams on pristine land.
Crystal shards in sunlight gleam,
Nature's breath in winter's dream.

Mountains rise with icy breath,
Guardians of the chill of death.
Whispers echo in the freeze,
Songs of silence, wild, and tease.

Every flake a story told,
In the shimmer, brave and bold.
Underneath the azure sky,
Glacial beauty will not die.

Rivers slow to crystal light,
In the shadows of the night.
Frozen patterns, art sublime,
Nature's canvas, pure in time.

As ages pass, the ice retreats,
Leaving trails where water meets.
Glimmers fade but memories stay,
In glacial hearts, a timeless play.

The Still Heart of a Winter Night

Silent stars in velvet skies,
Moonlight dances, softly sighs.
Snowflakes whisper, fall like dreams,
In the stillness, silence beams.

Frosty breath upon the air,
Echoes linger everywhere.
Nature wrapped in a soft shroud,
Calmness reigns, both fierce and proud.

Windows glow with firelight's grace,
Warmth within the chilly space.
Outside, shadows gently creep,
In the night's embrace, we sleep.

Branches bare, in stillness sway,
Underneath the moon's soft ray.
Every heartbeat feels so near,
In this moment, crystal clear.

Time stands still in cold delight,
As dreams dance in the winter night.
Wrapped in peace, a deepened sigh,
In this heart, the world goes by.

Frosty Inspirations

Delicate crystals on the ground,
Nature's art, a beauty found.
Every window paints a scene,
Frosty whispers, quiet green.

Icicles hang like silver threads,
Winter's gift on rooftops spreads.
With each step, a crunch, a sound,
In this magic, life abounds.

Breath of winter, fresh and bright,
Shadows dance in soft moonlight.
Ideas spark, as chill inspires,
Creativity in frozen fires.

Every flake a chance to dream,
In this cold, the heart will beam.
Nature's pause, a gentle nudge,
In the frost, our spirits budge.

From the cold, we find our way,
Turning night into the day.
Frosty inspirations rise,
From the chill, our passion flies.

Silent Reflections

In the stillness of the night,
Whispers dance in silver light.
Shadows weave through starry skies,
Echoes of forgotten sighs.

Beneath the moon's soft glowing beam,
Secrets linger like a dream.
Time stands still, a gentle pause,
Nature's beauty draws our cause.

Ripples on a tranquil pond,
Thoughts adrift, we wander fond.
Silent moments fill the air,
In this peace, we cease to care.

Reflections cast upon the stream,
Glimmers of a distant theme.
Every heartbeat, every breath,
Reminds us of the dance with death.

In twilight's embrace, we find rest,
Quiet minds, we are our best.
A sacred space where we belong,
In silent reflections, we grow strong.

The Quietude of Dusk

As daylight fades into warm hues,
Whispers of night begin to muse.
Crisp air wraps around the trees,
Rustling leaves in gentle breeze.

Shadows stretch, and colors blend,
Daylight sighs, and night attends.
Stars appear like distant eyes,
Watching over twilight skies.

Softly falls the evening's cloak,
In the hush, the world awoke.
Crickets sing their lullaby,
Underneath the starlit sky.

In the quiet, thoughts take flight,
Floating softly into night.
Embracing peace, we let go,
In the dusk's warm, gentle glow.

Time slows down, a soothing balm,
In this moment, we feel calm.
The quietude of dusk holds sway,
As worries gently fade away.

Frozen Horizons

In the stillness of winter's breath,
Frozen landscapes whisper death.
Blankets of white, so pure, so bright,
Hiding secrets, cloaked in light.

Mountains rise, their peaks aglow,
Where icy winds and cold winds flow.
Nature's art, both fierce and bold,
Stories of the past unfold.

Footprints trace a path anew,
Leading us where dreams come true.
Silence reigns, a sacred space,
Finding solace in this place.

The horizon glimmers, far from reach,
In frozen depth, the heart will teach.
Time stands still in winter's grasp,
In icy moments, we shall clasp.

With every breath, the world transformed,
In frozen beauty, we are warmed.
The horizon speaks of dreams in frost,
Boundless wishes, never lost.

A Tapestry of Frost

Delicate patterns lace the glass,
Nature's artwork, as time will pass.
Each crystal breath, a tale untold,
Wrapped in whispers, bright and bold.

Frosty fingers trace the air,
Crafting worlds beyond compare.
A tapestry of fleeting grace,
In winter's heart, we find our place.

Morning sunlight kisses the scene,
Glistening gems, a vibrant sheen.
Birds take flight, on wings of white,
Dancing freely in the light.

As the day unfolds its glow,
The tapestry begins to slow.
Nature sighs, a gentle breath,
In every moment, life and death.

Weaving memories, rich and vast,
In a canvas that will not last.
A tapestry of frost shall stay,
Etched in hearts, come what may.

The Flicker of Distant Fires

In twilight's gentle arms, they gleam,
Fires whisper tales from a passionate dream.
Through the haze, the colors play,
Embers dance, as night turns to day.

A silhouette of time takes flight,
Casting shadows in the fading light.
Each flicker holds a heartfelt sigh,
A bond of moments, soaring high.

Ghosts of laughter in the breeze,
Calling forth the memories with ease.
The warmth that lingers, softly shared,
In distant fires, true love declared.

Fleeting moments flicker and fade,
Yet in the heart, they're never swayed.
For every spark that graces the night,
Holds within it, the purest light.

So gaze into the dusk with care,
Let the glowing embers share.
The stories whispered on the wire,
Of hope and dreams in distant fire.

Murmurs of Ancient Chill

In valleys deep, where echoes hum,
The winter's breath has softly come.
A tapestry of frost and stone,
Whispers of ages, secrets known.

Each gentle sigh, a tale untold,
Of wandering hearts in the cold.
Beneath the stars, they scurry near,
The ancient chill, a haunting fear.

Amidst the trees, the shadows creep,
Where memories of time still sleep.
The branches sway, and spirits weave,
In the stillness, we believe.

The moonlight reflects on icy streams,
Where twilight holds the world's lost dreams.
Chill in the air, the night's soft call,
Within the silence, we feel it all.

So listen close, to the night's serenade,
The whispers of time that will not fade.
In ancient chill, we find our place,
In the heart of winter's warm embrace.

Sown in Solitude

In a garden where shadows play,
Seeds of solitude find their way.
Each whisper soft, each sigh profound,
In lonely soil, lost dreams are found.

Petals fall like gentle tears,
Carrying the weight of unspoken fears.
Yet from the earth, life starts to bloom,
In solitude, we cease our gloom.

The quiet embrace of the morning light,
Brings forth a promise, a hopeful sight.
A single flower, brave and bold,
Tells a story of hearts consoled.

Through solitude, we learn to grow,
To cultivate the love we sow.
With every season that comes and goes,
In the heart of stillness, compassion flows.

So tend the garden deep within,
Plant your dreams, let life begin.
For in solitude, we find our way,
A path to joy in every day.

Shimmering Shadows

In twilight's glow, the shadows dance,
A glimmering hint of a fleeting chance.
They sway and spin in playful delight,
Whispers of secrets beneath the night.

Against the backdrop of silent trees,
They move like echoes in the breeze.
Each shimmer tells of paths unseen,
Of wishes lost, and dreams between.

The silver light of the moon above,
Casts gentle warmth, a nudge of love.
In every flicker, the stories unfold,
Where shadows shimmer, and hearts are bold.

Like fleeting moments that soon will fade,
The shimmering shadows in twilight parade.
With every heartbeat, they sway and blend,
A tapestry woven, as time does bend.

So let us dance with shadows near,
Embrace the magic, feel no fear.
For in their glow, we find our way,
In shimmering shadows, come what may.

Nature's Tender Respite

In the forest's gentle sway,
Whispers of the leaves play,
Sunlight dances through the trees,
Breezes hum a soothing tease.

Wildflowers bloom in hues so bright,
Filling the air with pure delight,
Birds soar high on azure skies,
Nature's song, a sweet reprise.

Rivers babble with soft grace,
Reflecting all in their embrace,
Mountains stand in silent awe,
Guardians of the eternal law.

Each petal kissed by morning dew,
A canvas painted fresh and new,
In every corner, life unfolds,
A story only nature holds.

As twilight casts its golden hue,
Silent stars begin to strew,
In this tender, sacred space,
Nature's heart finds its embrace.

Soft Footprints on a White Canvas

Fresh snow blankets the silent ground,
In its embrace, beauty is found,
A world transformed with quiet grace,
Each trail marks a gentle trace.

Footprints left in frozen light,
Stories whisper, soft and bright,
Every step, a fleeting tale,
Carried forth on winter's gale.

Beneath the hush, life still stirs,
Hidden wonders, soft purrs,
Birds on branches, gently sway,
Nature's rhythm finds its way.

Crystals shimmer in moonlit glow,
A tapestry of white below,
In the stillness, dreams take flight,
As stars sprinkle the endless night.

With every breath, the cold air bites,
Yet warmth ignites in cozy nights,
Soft footprints lead to hearts anew,
In winter's arms, a love so true.

Hearts Kindled in the Frost

Amidst the chill of bitter winds,
Hearts ignite where warmth begins,
Fires crackle with stories told,
Around the flames, love unfolds.

Frozen landscapes, stark yet bright,
Every glimmer holds the light,
In shared laughter, spirits rise,
Kindled hearts beneath the skies.

As snowflakes dance in frosty air,
Moments linger, sweet and rare,
Holding hands in the tranquil night,
Together, we embrace the light.

The world outside may chill and freeze,
Yet love blooms in silent ease,
With every glance, a spark ignites,
Hearts united, reaching heights.

Through winter's grasp, we find our way,
In every dawn, a promise stays,
In the frost, our spirits soar,
Hearts kindled forevermore.

A Serenade of Silence

In the hush of distant hills,
Nature breathes, the spirit thrills,
Mountains echo a gentle tune,
Beneath the watchful silver moon.

Soft winds weave through branches tall,
A serenade, a soothing call,
Night's stillness wraps the world tight,
Whispers blend in soft twilight.

Stars peek through the velvet sky,
Each one holds a secret why,
A story sung not loud, but clear,
Silence speaks, and holds us near.

Moonlit paths guide our way home,
In the darkness, we freely roam,
With every breath, a tranquil sigh,
A serenade, a lullaby.

In this peace, our souls align,
With the universe, we intertwine,
In every heartbeat, silence reigns,
A serenade where love remains.

The Gentle Call of Frost

A breath of silence on the ground,
The world dressed in white all around.
Soft whispers echo through the trees,
Winter's touch brings a tender freeze.

Footprints linger, quiet and small,
Nature answers the gentle call.
Stars twinkle in the crystal night,
Guiding dreams with their soft light.

In this calm, hearts find their peace,
As time slows down and woes decrease.
The frosty air, a soothing balm,
Wraps the world in a soothing calm.

Snowflakes dance, a waltz so sweet,
Tracing patterns in the street.
Each moment frozen, a memory cast,
In the embrace of winter, unsurpassed.

When morning breaks, the sun will rise,
Painting warmth in the winter skies.
But for now, let the frost unfold,
A gentle story, softly told.

Whispers in the Chill

The moon hangs low in twilight's grace,
Casting shadows on a silent space.
Whispers travel on the winter air,
Secrets shared without a care.

Frosty breaths of night unwind,
Kissed by starlight, softly blind.
Trees stand tall in serene repose,
Guardians of the tales they chose.

Every sigh from the frozen ground,
Holds the echoes of love profound.
Chill embraces, a lover's kiss,
In the stillness, find your bliss.

Footsteps crunch on the icy crust,
Each sound a promise, a whispering trust.
Nature's lullaby, soft and low,
Guides us gently where we go.

Beneath the stars, the night unfolds,
Of dreams and stories, softly told.
So let us linger, hold this thrill,
Lost in the magic, whispers in the chill.

Lanterns of the Dark

In the shadows, lanterns glow,
Flickering flames in the night's flow.
Guiding wanderers back to light,
Through the silence, banishing fright.

Each step carries a hopeful spark,
Illuminating paths in the dark.
The whispers of light weave and play,
Leading hearts along the way.

Threads of gold in the midnight air,
A tapestry woven with utmost care.
Stories flicker in that gentle hue,
Shining softly, each one true.

The night stretches, vast and grand,
As lanterns offer a guiding hand.
Amidst the shadows, courage thrives,
For in the dark, true magic lives.

So gather round, share your tales,
As the soft light flickers and pales.
In the embrace of the night's sweet dream,
Lanterns flicker, a gentle beam.

Cradled in Cold Light

Wrapped in blankets, warm and tight,
We find solace in the cold light.
Stars above like diamonds shine,
Cradling dreams, yours and mine.

The world outside, a frozen art,
Whispers of winter touch the heart.
Stillness hugs the night so tight,
As moonbeams dance in soft twilight.

Beneath the branches, snowflakes fall,
A gentle hush, a sacred call.
Nature cradles the earth in white,
Holding us close in cold light.

Each breath we take, a cloud in air,
Sparkling secrets, moments rare.
Time stands still, dreams take flight,
In this embrace, everything's right.

So let us breathe in this quiet grace,
In the cold light, find our place.
Cradled in wonder, together we'll stay,
Until the dawn breaks the night away.

The Quiet of Chilled Afternoons

The air hangs still, a whispered sigh,
Beneath the sky, where shadows lie.
Frost clings tight to barren trees,
In silence wrapped, a sense of ease.

The warmth of sun is far away,
Yet heartbeats pulse in soft ballet.
Each breath a cloud, each step a dance,
In this still world, I find my trance.

Branches creak, a subtle sound,
With every echo, peace is found.
Time slows down, the world seems new,
As quiet settles, calm and true.

Colors fade, the day retreats,
In softening light, the evening greets.
Chilled afternoons in muted tones,
As day ends gently, I am home.

Underneath the twilight glow,
Memories whisper from below.
Wrapped in stillness, dreams take flight,
In the quiet of the fading light.

Sprigs of Life Beneath the Ice

Hidden well beneath the cold,
Life awaits, a tale untold.
Gentle shoots in slumber lay,
Whispering spring is on the way.

Crystals form like ancient shields,
Yet beneath, the earth still yields.
Nature's cycle, soft and slow,
Life awakens from its snow.

The frost may grip with summer's threat,
But deep within, the seeds are set.
Each stem a promise, dear and bright,
To break the chill, to seek the light.

Beneath the ice, the world holds breath,
In quiet hope, defying death.
Nature knows the dance of time,
Awakening in rhythm, prime.

So here we wait through winter's reign,
For life to stir and break the chain.
In every sprig, the promise lies,
Of vibrant blooms and clearer skies.

Twilight in the Snowdrifts

Twilight whispers, soft as snow,
The world is hushed, a calming glow.
Drifts of white in twilight's hold,
Stories written, yet untold.

Footprints vanish, lost in time,
Layered silence, pure and prime.
Sky above a canvas deep,
In winter's arms, the world does sleep.

Shadows stretch and colors blend,
The day bids night, its gentle friend.
Stars blink awake in cobalt skies,
As quiet falls, the night complies.

In these drifts, dreams take form,
A frosty world, serene and warm.
Moments linger, caught in flight,
In twilight's grasp, all feels right.

Hold this peace, let worries fade,
In the magic of dusk's parade.
The snowdrifts cradle dreams and sighs,
As night wraps gently, calm and wise.

Crystals of an Unseen Future

Glimmers lie within the dark,
Each facet holds a hidden spark.
Crystals forming, bright and clear,
Hope suspended, drawing near.

In frozen depths where shadows creep,
Future's promise starts to seep.
Under layers of ice and stone,
New beginnings, quietly grown.

Time stands still in this enchanted place,
Holding dreams in soft embrace.
With every heartbeat, futures bloom,
In silence, break through winter's gloom.

Each crystal veils a tale untold,
Of destinies and dreams bold.
The unseen threads that bind the fates,
Beneath the frost, the heart awaits.

So let us wait, let patience reign,
For beauty often hides in pain.
In the crystal's grasp, we'll find our truth,
Unlocking secrets, the gift of youth.

Dreams Beneath the Snow

Whispers of dreams in frosty air,
Softly they linger, light as despair.
Beneath the snow, secrets reside,
Where hope and silence gently collide.

Blanketed thoughts in winter's embrace,
Chasing the warmth of a fleeting place.
Stars glisten bright in the endless night,
Guiding the dreams that take fragile flight.

Footprints erased by the icy breath,
Each step a story that dances with death.
In hushed tones, the world comes alive,
As visions awaken, we dare to strive.

Amidst the chill, passions may grow,
Igniting the fire that longs to glow.
In every snowflake, a promise is spun,
Dreams beneath the snow have only begun.

So let the winter wrap you in grace,
Drawing the warmth from time's gentle face.
For in this stillness, dreams can be sown,
And in the heart, they will always be known.

Resting Under a Blanket

Tucked beneath layers, warmth surrounds,
A gentle embrace in peaceful sounds.
The world outside a distant tune,
Under a blanket, we drift to noon.

With whispering winds that softly play,
Time stands still on this cozy day.
Each breath a moment, slow and deep,
In this cocoon, the heart can leap.

Stories unfold in flickering light,
Casting shadows that dance through the night.
Memories linger, tales softly spun,
Under the blanket, we are one.

Here lies comfort, the world fades away,
Wrapped in love, blissfully we stay.
Dreams intertwine like threads in a seam,
Resting together, lost in a dream.

Let the hours melt like a sweet refrain,
Echoing softly, like gentle rain.
Under this blanket, wherever we roam,
Is a sanctuary, a feeling of home.

The Stillness of Time

In the hush of twilight, moments suspend,
Where the heart and the cosmos beautifully blend.
Each tick of the clock, a fragile thread,
In the stillness of time, all worries shed.

Colors unfurl in a soft, whispered tone,
As shadows stretch out, the world feels alone.
Yet in this solitude, peace takes its hold,
Revealing the stories that silence has told.

The air, full of magic, carries the weight,
Of dreams and desires that patiently wait.
In the stillness, whispers become our guide,
Leading us gently where hopes can abide.

Moments of stillness, sweetly we crave,
Building our courage on the lives that we brave.
For time, when embraced, often bends and breaks,
In that quiet space, the soul quietly wakes.

So let us breathe in these fleeting shades,
Finding our solace where silence cascades.
In the stillness of time, we learn to be free,
Discovering truth in our shared memory.

Shimmering Possibilities

Glimmers of hope like stars in the night,
Dance through the darkness, igniting the light.
Each spark a whisper of dreams yet untold,
Shimmering possibilities begin to unfold.

With every heartbeat, the universe sings,
The promise of magic that each moment brings.
In the quiet, we feel our spirits take flight,
Guided by visions that twinkle so bright.

The canvas of life paints colors anew,
As shadows dissolve, revealing what's true.
From the depths of our hearts, visions arise,
In shimmering possibilities, we find the skies.

With courage to chase what the future can yield,
In fields of desire, our dreams are revealed.
The journey of living begins with a spark,
Lighting our paths in the vast, endless dark.

So dare to embrace what your heart truly knows,
In the tapestry woven, let your spirit pose.
For every possibility blooms like a flower,
Shimmering bright in the twilight hour.

Nestled Beneath the Stars

In the quiet of the night,
Whispers of dreams take flight.
The skies adorned with light,
A tapestry of delight.

Softly glows the silver moon,
Crickets sing a gentle tune.
Nature breathes in sweet cocoon,
Embracing all, none too soon.

Underneath the starry veil,
Hopeful hearts begin to sail.
In this peace, we shall prevail,
A timeless, enchanting tale.

Wrapped in warmth, the night unfolds,
As constellations brightly hold.
Secrets of the night retold,
In every shimmer, magic bold.

Together we will gaze and dream,
In the dark, our spirits beam.
With every sigh, a shared theme,
A world woven in love's seam.

Heartbeats Beneath the Snow

Frosty whispers in the air,
Snowflakes dance without a care.
Silent streets, a tranquil stare,
Winter's breath is everywhere.

Hearts entwined beneath the chill,
With warmth that time cannot distill.
In the stillness, love does thrill,
With gentle pulses, we fulfill.

Tracks of footsteps, secrets shared,
In the cold, two souls have dared.
Every moment, love ensnared,
In the snow, we are repaired.

Glowing embers from within,
Against the cold, our hearts begin.
In this season, love's sweet sin,
Every heartbeat echoes in.

As stars peek through the winter gray,
We find warmth in the night's display.
Hand in hand, we drift and sway,
In the snow, love lights our way.

Tales from the Icy Realm

In an icy land, so bold,
Stories of the past unfold.
Frozen rivers, wonders told,
Magic weaves through every fold.

Whispers of the ancient trees,
Breezes hum in harmonies.
Every flake, a mystery,
Nature's voice, a symphony.

Mountains rise with tales to share,
Frosty giants, standing rare.
Crystalled dreams embracing air,
In their shadows, we declare.

Echoes of the wild are near,
Through the frost, we have no fear.
In our hearts, we hold what's dear,
In the ice, a path is clear.

With every glance, the magic swells,
In the silence, history dwells.
Underneath the winter's spells,
Tales from frozen depths compel.

Moonlit Frost

Beneath the glow of moonlit frost,
Dreams awaken, never lost.
In the night, we count the cost,
Finding warmth in what's embossed.

A silver sheen upon the ground,
In the stillness, peace is found.
Nature sleeps, a whispered sound,
Yet in hearts, love is profound.

Stars like diamonds, bright and clear,
In this moment, we draw near.
Each breath shared, a reason dear,
Underneath the skies sincere.

Frost-kissed dreams upon our skin,
With every heartbeat, we begin.
In this night, two souls will spin,
Moonlit magic deep within.

In the shadow of the night,
Love ignites, a dazzling light.
Through the chill, our hearts take flight,
In the frost, we find our right.

A Dance of Ice and Dreams

Whispers of winter swirl in the air,
Glittering frost captures dreams laid bare.
Moonlight dances on a frozen stream,
Echoes of magic ignite every beam.

Footprints fade in a shimmering lace,
Each step a secret, a timeless embrace.
Stars above twinkle with ancient glee,
In this waltz of wonder, just you and me.

Shadows cast soft on the glistening ground,
Echoes of laughter, a joyous sound.
With every twirl, the world drifts away,
In the dance of ice, we long to stay.

Glistening crystals, a tapestry bright,
Painting our hearts with enchanting light.
Lost in the moment, we soar and glide,
In a dream fulfilled, where spirits reside.

As winter's breath cradles the night,
Our dreams take flight in the pale starlight.
Together we weave this spellbinding scheme,
In the dance of ice, we awaken a dream.

Frost-kissed Resilience

In the heart of winter, where silence reigns,
Nature's beauty glistens, breaking chains.
Frost-kissed petals hold tales untold,
Life's quiet strength in each shimmer of cold.

Beneath the surface lies a fierce glow,
Roots intertwining where resilience flows.
Against the harsh winds and icy snare,
Life finds a way, a constant prayer.

Each morning rises with new hope in sight,
Sunshine breaking through the deep frozen night.
The world may slumber, but beneath the snow,
A pulse of life whispers, ready to grow.

With every storm, the trees stand tall,
Branches weathering, they heed the call.
Frost-kissed resilience carved in the bark,
Carrying stories, a strength from the dark.

So let us gather, in warmth of the fire,
Celebrate spirit that won't tire.
In frost and in chill, we find our song,
Resilience blooms where we all belong.

Beneath a Shroud of Snow

Veils of white drape the earth so sweet,
Whispers of silence beneath our feet.
Every flake tells a story so pure,
Under this shroud, tranquility's lure.

Branches bowed low with a frosted crest,
Nature's canvas shows only the best.
Hidden beneath lies the promise of spring,
A world transformed, awaiting its fling.

In the hush of the twilight, peace unfolds,
Secrets of winter, tenderly told.
Beneath the surface, life quietly dreams,
In the stillness, hearts find their beams.

Footsteps are muffled, the air crisp and bright,
A world embraced in ethereal light.
Though cold may linger, warmth starts to glow,
Hope arises, beneath a shroud of snow.

Embrace the stillness, let worries drift,
In this moment, savor the gift.
For seasons will change, their cycles bestow,
A magic alive beneath a shroud of snow.

Tranquil Reveries

In soft twilight, the world slows down,
Wrapped in colors of lavender crown.
Whispers of dreams float in the air,
Painting the silence with gentle care.

Out on the lake, reflections flutter,
Leaves dance lightly, no words to utter.
As shadows stretch, the sky ignites,
Each fleeting moment, endless delights.

Beneath the stars, our worries cease,
Wrapped in the night, we find our peace.
Fragrant blooms rise with the moon's soft rise,
Tranquility lingers, a soothing prize.

Each sigh of the breeze, a calming note,
In nature's embrace, our spirits float.
Together we weave these tranquil themes,
Lost in the magic of tender dreams.

As dawn approaches with grace and light,
We carry these moments, forever bright.
In the swells of life, we remain free,
In tranquil reveries, just you and me.

Dreams Wrapped in Flakes

Softly fall the winter's gift,
Whispers dance in frosty air.
Each flake holds a silent wish,
Floating dreams beyond compare.

Children laugh, their spirits soar,
While snowflakes twirl in swirling flight.
Magic drapes the world in white,
As evening falls, the stars ignite.

A cozy world, with joy entwined,
Light the fires, let warmth arise.
In slumber's arms, we find our peace,
As dreams drift softly, like the skies.

Outside, the chill begins to bite,
Inside, a glow that feels so right.
With every flake, many stories told,
In winter nights, both young and old.

Boundless dreams in icy lace,
Embrace the night, let hearts be free.
Together we find our sacred space,
In snow's embrace, the world we see.

A Time to Hibernate

Nature sleeps in blankets deep,
Quiet woods in silence dwell.
Animals rest, their secrets keep,
While frost adorns each frozen bell.

Branches bare, under grey skies,
Winter whispers, soft and low.
Time to pause, to close our eyes,
And find the warmth where embers glow.

Beneath the earth, roots intertwine,
Nurtured dreams through icy gloom.
A cycle turns, all will align,
In time, we'll bloom from winter's tomb.

Stars above like ancient eyes,
Guide us through the darkest days.
Resting hearts, beneath the skies,
In quiet nights, we find our ways.

Together we will rise anew,
As spring awakens life once more.
With hope renewed and skies so blue,
In time's embrace, our spirits soar.

Stillness in the Cold

A blanket white over fields so wide,
Stillness holds the breath of dawn.
Footprints left where shadows hide,
In the chill, the world feels drawn.

Icicles hang like crystal tears,
Every breath a cloud of mist.
Nature's hush throughout the years,
In frozen beauty, we exist.

Branches creak under weight so pure,
The air is crisp, it bites and stings.
Yet in this cold, there's warmth obscure,
Where love and laughter always sings.

Moments freeze in timeless grace,
As winter paints its silent story.
In every flake, a sacred space,
In every heart, a hidden glory.

Let us wander through the night,
With fingers tugged in pockets warm.
Find in stillness, pure delight,
As winter weaves its gentle charm.

The Hearth's Gentle Glow

A crackling fire, soft and bright,
Leaps and dances in the dark.
Flickers warm, a welcome sight,
Embers glow, igniting spark.

Family gathered, tales unfold,
In winter's grip, we share our dreams.
With every laugh, the warmth takes hold,
Binding hearts like flowing streams.

Sipping cocoa, flavors rich,
Time drifts slowly, moments blend.
In this glow, we find the niche,
Where every heart can safely mend.

Outside, the snow falls soft and light,
Inside, the love ignites the air.
In this space, all feels just right,
Where memories are made to share.

When shadows stretch and silence reigns,
The hearth's embrace, forever near.
We hold on tight to love's old chains,
In winter's warmth, we find our cheer.

Frozen Reflections

In the mirror of ice, dreams lie,
Silent whispers of time gone by.
Captured moments, glints of light,
A world transformed, soft and white.

Each breath a cloud in the frozen air,
Nature's stillness, a canvas rare.
Beneath the frost, life still flows,
Hidden stories nature knows.

Crisp branches sparkle, a jeweled crown,
Every flake, a soft gentle frown.
Shadows dance in the pale moon glow,
In frozen reflections, secrets flow.

The chill invites a warm embrace,
While winter paints with delicate grace.
The echo of footsteps in layered snow,
Retracing paths where soft winds blow.

In silence deep, the heart finds peace,
A quiet moment where worries cease.
Frozen reflections, a calm retreat,
In nature's hand, our souls meet.

Warmth in the Still

Amidst the frost, a fire ignites,
A beacon glowing through cold nights.
Embers crackle, stories untold,
In the warmth, memories unfold.

The world outside, a tranquil sight,
Yet here we gather, hearts alight.
With laughter shared and voices near,
In the stillness, love is clear.

The chill may bite, but not our hearts,
For in this glow, the magic starts.
Each sip of cocoa, sweet delight,
Warms our spirits through the night.

Outside, the snow drapes the ground,
Yet inside, joy and peace abound.
In this cocoon where love can sway,
We find warmth in the still of day.

Fingers clasped, stories blend,
With every moment, we transcend.
As stars peek through the frosty veil,
Warmth in the still will always prevail.

Hushed Paths of Snow

Through hushed paths where silence reigns,
Nature whispers in soft refrains.
Footprints fade in the soft, white crust,
In snowy embrace, we learn to trust.

The trees stand tall, cloaked in white,
Guardians of secrets held tight.
Each breath released, a moment caught,
In the quiet, solace is sought.

Winds gently weave through branches bare,
A lullaby floats in the crisp air.
Together we wander, lost in thought,
On hushed paths, what we've sought.

With every step, the world transforms,
A tranquil place where peace conforms.
In this stillness, hearts can know,
The beauty found in paths of snow.

The landscape glimmers, a silent hymn,
As twilight shades the horizon dim.
In the hush, where echoes belong,
Paths of snow lead us along.

A Tapestry of White

Across the hills, a blanket spreads,
A tapestry of white, life treads.
Each flake a stitch in winter's quilt,
Woven stories where shadows are spilt.

In morning's glow, the crystals gleam,
A world untouched, as if in a dream.
With every drift, new tales are spun,
A canvas bright beneath the sun.

Beneath the surface, life still breathes,
In every layer, nature weaves.
The laughter of children breaks the calm,
As snowballs fly, a fleeting balm.

Evening whispers a soft embrace,
The stars emerge in the quiet space.
In this moment, time seems to pause,
A tapestry of white for us to cause.

Under the frost, the earth will renew,
In every season, life will construe.
But for now, we revel in wonder and light,
Wrapped in the warmth of a tapestry bright.

The Gentle Hand of Cold

The winter whispers soft and low,
A tender touch, the world in snow.
Each flake a secret, softly spun,
A quiet peace when day is done.

Branches wear a crystal crown,
Veils of white upon the brown.
Stars twinkle in the frosted night,
Guiding dreams with silver light.

Hushed are footsteps, sounds subdued,
In this realm of icy mood.
Nature's breath, a misty sigh,
Underneath the slate gray sky.

Frozen streams like glass do gleam,
Reflecting all the night's sweet dream.
Life awaits with patient grace,
In the chill, a warm embrace.

The gentle hand, it holds us tight,
Cradled safe through darkest night.
So let the cold envelop me,
In its arms, I feel so free.

Petals of Ice and Hope

In the garden of winter's breath,
Emerges beauty, defying death.
Petals glimmer like diamond tears,
Whispers of spring that hold our fears.

Each flower forged in icy flame,
Fragile dreams, they play their game.
Hope unfolds with the morning light,
A promise kept in the coldest night.

Crystal leaves upon the ground,
Nature's art, so profound.
Glistening softly, they beg to stay,
In the heart, where warmth finds a way.

Veils of frost in the early dawn,
Shimmering brightly, life reborn.
With every breath, we find our way,
Through the chill of a brand new day.

Hope entwined with fragile ice,
In their beauty, we find paradise.
As seasons turn and time does flow,
Our hearts will bloom with petals of hope.

Woodland Sentinels in White

Ancient trees clad in winter's gown,
Guardians of the silent town.
Their branches stretch toward the sky,
In solemn peace, they stand nearby.

Snowflakes dance on the forest floor,
A blanket soft, forever more.
Underneath the tranquil dome,
Nature finds her quiet home.

Whispers echo through the trees,
Carried gently by the breeze.
Creatures pause in awe and thrill,
In the realm of winter's chill.

Each trunk a tale of time once known,
In white they wear the seeds they've sown.
Woodland sentinels stand so tall,
Witnesses to the beauty of it all.

Frosted whispers, secrets shared,
In this sanctuary, we are spared.
Under their watch, we find our place,
A moment of peace, a warm embrace.

An Ode to the Frost

Ode to the frost that graces morn,
In delicate patterns, softly born.
Each icy breath, a work of art,
A timeless dance, an ache of heart.

Kissed by the dawn's first gentle light,
A glistening world, so pure and bright.
Nature's palette, a shining white,
A canvas stretched, a wondrous sight.

On the window, it paints a scene,
An intricate spell, serene and clean.
The world outside feels far away,
In this frosty embrace, we pray.

With every breath, we shiver slow,
In the grip of winter's flow.
But in the chill, our hearts ignite,
For warmth is found in love's sweet light.

So here's to the frost, the cold's design,
A moment to cherish, a place divine.
An ode we sing to winter's grace,
In its whiteness, we find our space.

Frost-Kissed Promises

In the dawn's gentle glow,
Whispers dance on the breeze,
Frost-kissed leaves aglow,
Promises held with ease.

Silent nights cloak the trees,
Each branch a wondrous sight,
Nature's soft melodies,
Brought forth by the cold light.

Frozen rivers meander,
Carving paths through the land,
Hearts feel a sweet candor,
While warmth takes gentle stand.

Beneath stars that shimmer,
Dreams float like clouds above,
A moment that won't wither,
Wrapped in the chill of love.

As dawn breaks the starlit charms,
The frost begins to fade,
Yet memories held in arms,
Will never know how they're made.

Shadows of Snowfall

In the quiet of night's shroud,
Soft flakes drift in the air,
Whispers under the cloud,
Blanketing all with care.

Footsteps crunch on the ground,
A dance in purest white,
Each shadow spun around,
Casts dreams of pure delight.

Moonlight bathes the still trees,
Flickers on icy streams,
Nature hums with a breeze,
Singing our frozen dreams.

Laughter mixes with chill,
As we play in this art,
Time pauses, soft and still,
Filling each joyful heart.

As dawn breaks the twilight veil,
With colors bold and bright,
The shadows start to pale,
But the memories ignite.

Embracing the Frost

In the morning's cool embrace,
I find solace in the chill,
Nature wears a frozen face,
Yet it gives my heart a thrill.

Each breath hangs in the air,
A crystal dance of delight,
Frosty whispers everywhere,
Guiding me through the night.

Branches heavy with pearls,
Drifting diamonds in the sun,
Amidst this world that twirls,
I know my heart has won.

As the day begins to wane,
And shadows stretch and flee,
I'll cherish this sweet strain,
Of frost that sets me free.

With night falling soft and deep,
The stars begin to gleam,
In this silence, secrets seep,
Filling my heart with dream.

Secrets in the Frozen Night

Beneath the pale moonlight,
Secrets drape the land,
Wrapped in a frosty bite,
A truth we understand.

Each breath forms a cloud,
Memories glimmer and shine,
In this silence loud,
Every moment is divine.

The world whispers low,
A hush that fills the air,
In the soft, falling snow,
Answers linger everywhere.

While shadows dance and sway,
I find warmth in the cold,
This night will gently stay,
With tales waiting to be told.

As dawn starts to unfold,
And secrets melt away,
The beauty we behold,
Will linger through the day.

Lullabies for the Frozen

The moon whispers soft in the night,
Blankets of snow hold the world tight.
Stars twinkle like dreams in a trance,
Nature sleeps on, lost in a dance.

Whispers of chill brush through the trees,
Gentle and calm as a cool breeze.
Lullabies echo through the frost,
Memories linger but never lost.

In the stillness, a soft sigh flows,
Caressing the earth, where silence grows.
Each flake that falls writes a new tale,
In winter's embrace, where hearts prevail.

Time seems to pause in the frozen hue,
Wrapped in a dream, so pure and true.
Lullabies hum in the air so clear,
Cradled in warmth, we have no fear.

As night deepens and shadows blend,
Nature's lullabies softly extend.
Rest now, dear world, in tranquility,
For dreams await in the frozen sea.

Crystalline Hopes

In a world of ice, dreams take flight,
Crystalline hopes glimmer in the night.
Each frozen breath a whisper of light,
Reflecting the stars, oh so bright.

Glistening paths wound through the trees,
Carving the silence, carried by breeze.
Ice mirrors echo the dreams we keep,
Awakening wishes from winter's deep.

Frost-kissed petals, a delicate sight,
Promise of spring in the still of the night.
Hope dances softly on glimmering ground,
In the quiet, the magic is found.

Every flake a story, each twinkle a dream,
Flowing like rivers, a silvered seam.
Crystalline hopes rise with the dawn,
Awakening hearts as the dark is gone.

Though cold may linger, warmth will prevail,
Whispers of spring on a soft, gentle trail.
Crystalline hopes beneath the pale glow,
Awaiting the sun, where the blossoms will grow.

Beneath the Silver Sky

Under a blanket of silver and blue,
Dreams drift gently, as if on cue.
Stars hang low, their whispers so bright,
Guiding the lost through the velvet night.

A stillness reigns in the air so pure,
A secret held in the heart's allure.
Beneath the silver sky we find grace,
Time slows down in this sacred space.

Snowflakes flutter like dancers in flight,
Weaving a tapestry, sparkling light.
Echoes of laughter on crisp, cold air,
Moments of joy, beyond compare.

As shadows lengthen 'neath the dusting white,
A fire flickers, warming the night.
Stories emerge like stars that gleam,
Whispers of hope in the chill's soft dream.

Beneath the silver sky we are free,
Caught in the magic of winter's spree.
Together we stand, hearts open wide,
Embracing the peace that the season hides.

Songs of the Snowbound

In the hush of night, snowflakes fall,
Silent songs, nature's call.
Soft and pure, they blanket the ground,
A symphony played without a sound.

Whispers of winter weave through the trees,
Carried along by the frozen breeze.
Songs of the snowbound fill the air,
Notes of tranquility, floating with care.

Each flake a note in the winter's song,
A melody sweet where we all belong.
Beneath the stars, in this frosty embrace,
Harmony dwells in the silent space.

Fires crackle, illuminating the dark,
Hearts warm and bright, igniting a spark.
In this moment, we gather as one,
Singing the praises of winter's sun.

As echoes drift through the nighttime air,
We cherish the warmth, the love we share.
Songs of the snowbound, a timeless delight,
Filling our souls with the joy of the night.

Chill of Anticipation

The wind whispers low, a breath of the night,
Stars twinkle above, bathed in silver light.
Leaves rustle softly, a dance in the dark,
Promises linger, igniting a spark.

Frosty air nips, teasing the skin,
Morning will break; a new day begins.
Hearts beat in rhythm, as shadows grow long,
In the chill of the night, we find where we belong.

Laughter floats softly, echoing clear,
Each moment cherished, held close and dear.
A world wrapped in silence, untouched by the noise,
In the chill of anticipation, we find our joys.

Clouds gather slowly, a blanket of gray,
Whispers of winter, they tempt and they sway.
The horizon awaits, cloaked in allure,
We breathe in the magic, a feeling so pure.

As the dusk settles in, with a blanket of peace,
The chill wraps us tightly, a comforting fleece.
Together we stand, hearts open and wide,
In this wonderment, we shall abide.

Frosted Whispers

In the still of the morning, the world holds its breath,
Silence reigns deep, between life and death.
Frosted whispers linger, etched on each leaf,
Nature's soft canvas, a tale of belief.

The sun stretches slowly, breaking the chill,
Each ray a promise, a warmth to instill.
Glistening crystals dance upon ground,
A sparkling treasure, in silence, is found.

The trees wear their coats, a shimmery white,
Guardians of secrets, framing the light.
Footprints are captured, in snow and in ice,
Each step tells a story, simple yet nice.

Branches sway gently, a lullaby's charm,
Nature sings softly, a whisper of balm.
In the heart of the frost, dreams come alive,
Together we wander, in wonder we thrive.

As twilight descends, colors bleed and fade,
The world wrapped in stillness, a tranquil cascade.
Frosted whispers echo, as shadows take flight,
In this sacred silence, we embrace the night.

Veil of White

Beneath the soft veil, the earth slumbers deep,
A blanket of white, where silence does seep.
The world wears a crown, dazzling and bright,
In the calm of the evening, kissed by the light.

Snowflakes like feathers fall softly around,
Each one unique, in silence they're found.
The air is electric, a feeling divine,
In the grip of this moment, all hearts intertwine.

Shadows stretch long, as twilight unfolds,
The secrets of winter in whispers retold.
With each frosty breath, a promise awakens,
A dance in the white, where dreams are unshaken.

The night holds its treasures, as stars gleam above,
In the veil of pure white, we find what we love.
Wrapped in the magic, the quiet, the peace,
In this wintry cocoon, our spirits find ease.

With every soft flutter, the world feels alive,
In the heart of this white, our souls can derive.
A tapestry woven, by moonlight's embrace,
In the veil of white, we find our true place.

Echoes of a Silent Season

Quiet descends, as the earth breathes slow,
A canvas of white, where soft breezes flow.
Echoes of stillness, a whispered refrain,
In the heart of the woods, peace reigns once again.

Footsteps grow muffled, as shadows take form,
Nature's own lullaby, calming and warm.
Branches are bare, yet beauty remains,
In this silent season, life's joy has no chains.

The crackle of frost, a song on the breeze,
Every breath a treasure, as we move with ease.
Moments of wonder, in peace we reside,
In echoes of silence, our hearts open wide.

Snow-dusted pathways, inviting and clear,
Guide us to places where love conquers fear.
In the cold of the season, we find fiery light,
Echoes of warmth amid long winter nights.

As the twilight beckons, with stars shining down,
We gather our dreams, as night wears a crown.
In echoes of silence, our spirits connect,
In the heart of the season, we nurture respect.